Schaum
Making Music Method
Level Five

By John W. Schaum
Revised and Edited by Wesley Schaum

FOREWORD

The Schaum *Making Music Method* uses the proven middle-C approach integrated with ear, eye and finger training. This edition is the product of many years of teaching experience and continuing evaluation. Many careful refinements enhance the original pedagogic concepts.

Level Five widens musical horizons with new technical challenges and a variety of composers, pianistic styles and musical periods. This book presents rapidly repeated notes, the martellato accent, chromatic scale, reading a 3-staff vocal score, the turn, soft pedal, tremolo, reading a 4-part vocal score, 32nd notes, melody and accompaniment in the same hand, the whole tone scale and mordents.

Music appreciation and repertoire development are enhanced with presentations of program music, the tarantella, a waltz medley, comparison of opera and oratorio and the 2-part invention. Numerous transcriptions have been made from operatic, vocal and chamber music literature.

Self-help is encouraged by the inclusion of *Reference Pages* (front and rear inside covers) and a *Music Dictionary* (page 46). The student can sound out pronunciations of musical terms by using the phonetic syllables provided.

The Schaum *Making Music Method* consists of **eight books**, from Primer Level through Level 7.

Schaum Publications, Inc.
10235 N. Port Washington Rd. • Mequon, WI 53092
www.schaumpiano.net

01-36
AZ-25

CONTENTS

Schaum's Curriculum for Musicianship Development

Student musicianship is developed by a balanced curriculum that includes:
- Note Reading and Music Theory
- Finger Strength and Dexterity
- Music Appreciation and Repertoire Development

These practical supplementary books help to achieve musicianship goals.

Theory
Interval Speller
Chord Speller

Improvising
Easy Keyboard Harmony, Bk. 4

See page 48 for Sheet Music

Technic
Fingerpower, Level 5

Music for Fun
Boogie Is My Beat
Scott Joplin Ragtime, Bk. 1
Scott Joplin Ragtime, Bk. 2

Music Appreciation and Repertoire
American Sonatinas
Best of Chopin
Christmas Solos, Level 5
Handel's Messiah
Original Piano Classics for Level 5
Peer Gynt Suites
Sacred Solos, Level 5

All books are published and copyrighted by Schaum Publications, Inc. – www.schaumpiano.net

World's Fair

Presto ♩ = 88-100

*Moszkowski, Op. 23 No. 6

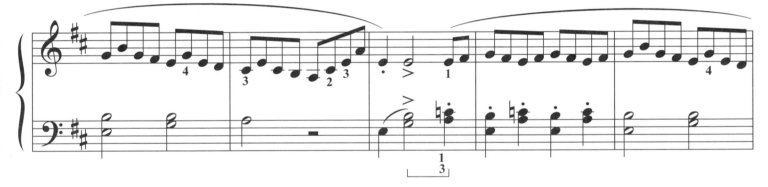

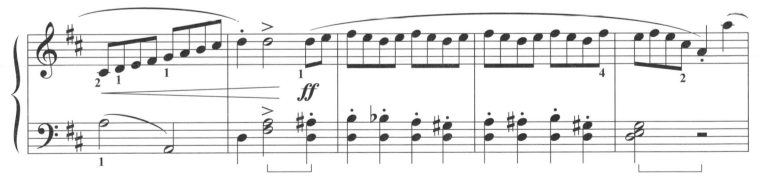

*Moritz Moszkowski (muss-KUFF-skee) Polish composer (1854-1925)

French Poodle

This piece is an example of **program music**, a style of writing in which a piece depicts a story, mood or action suggested by the title, such as the trotting and barking of the poodle in this piece.

John W. Schaum

* D.S. is the abbreviation of *dal segno* (dahl SEN-yoh), meaning go back to the sign 𝄋 and repeat until *Fine* (end).

Swiss Music Box

To produce the delicate effect of a tinkling music box, several new musical signs are used.

ppp = pianississimo (pee-an-nih-SISS-ee-moh) means extremely soft.

una corda (OO-nah KOHR-dah) means to use the soft pedal. The soft pedal is the pedal at the left of every piano. It is played with the left foot.

tre corde (TRAY KOHR-deh) means to release the soft pedal

15ma means to play two octaves higher than written (15 keys higher).

Tranquillo ♩ = 116-126

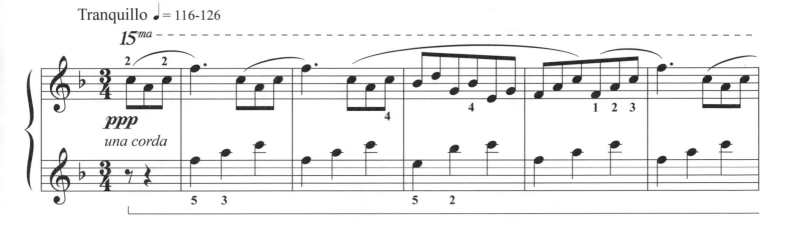

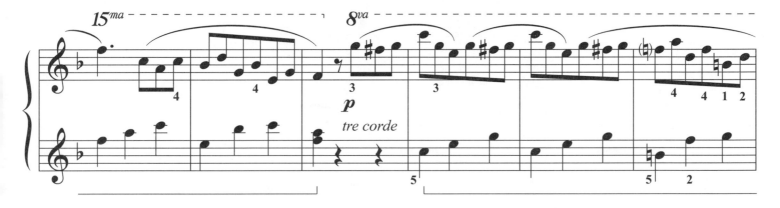

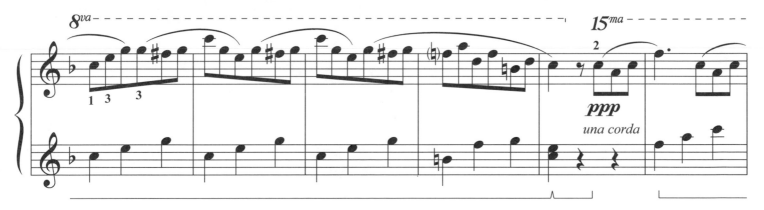

Dancers of Taranto

The **tarantella** is an Italian folk dance in six-eight time. The word is derived from the tarantula spider. It is named after the city of Taranto in southern Italy where the large European wolf spider was first found. A popular legend says that the fever produced by the poisonous bite of the tarantula can be cured by whirling round and round to the wild dance of the tarantella.

Vivace ♩. = 120-132

Beaumont

Suggested workbook: **Schaum CHORD SPELLER** (catalog #02-35) – Teaches analysis of triads and 7th chords.

Woodpecker's Waltz

Rapid Repeated Notes – When playing repeated notes in a fast tempo, it helps to change fingers on each note. For example, at the beginning of this piece the right hand uses the fingering: 4-3-2-1-3-2-1. Using this type of fingering avoids muscular tension and enables you to play the notes more distinctly.

*Ernest Gillet

* Ernest Gillet (1856-1940) French composer of light music. He was educated at the Paris Conservatory and played cello in the Paris Opera orchestra.

Patio Polka

> *Martellato* (mahr-tel-LAH-toh) is indicated with a small wedge shaped mark (▾) placed over or under a note head. It means to play with a heavy, hammer-like staccato touch.

Moderato ♩ = 92-100

Johann Strauss, Op. 117
(1825-1899)

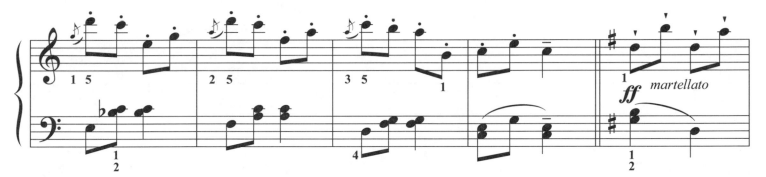

Neapolitan Serenade

Notice the special fingering at the end of the 2nd measure for the left hand. Finger number 1 is printed twice, one number above the other. The two numbers are connected with a bracket. This means that *both notes* are to be played *with the thumb*.

*Enrico Toselli

Andante ♩= 66-72

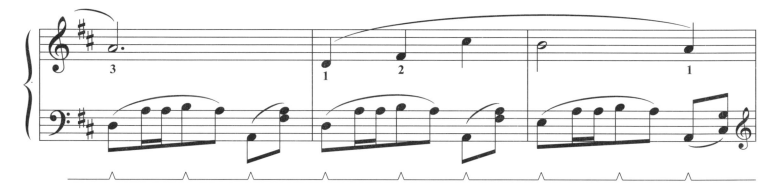

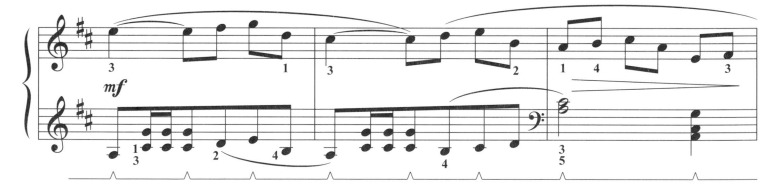

* Enrico Toselli (toe-ZELL-ee) Italian concert pianist and composer of operettas, piano music and songs (1883-1926). This piece is transcribed from his best-known song, originally written in 1900 for voice with piano accompaniment.

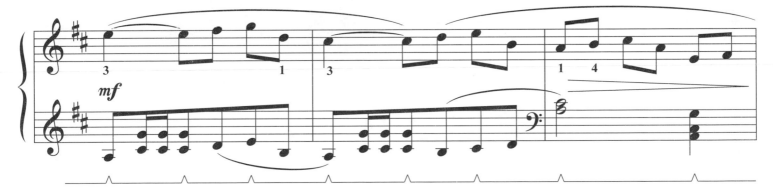

Suggested supplementary book for a contrast of style: **Boogie Is My Beat** (catalog #03-05)

Police Sirens At Night

This piece features the **chromatic scale**, built entirely of half steps. In general, the 3rd finger is used to play black keys. The damper pedal creates a blurred effect like the wail of the siren.

Vivace ♩ = 96-108

Water Under the Bridge

Andantino ♩ = 80-88

*Jessie L. Gaynor

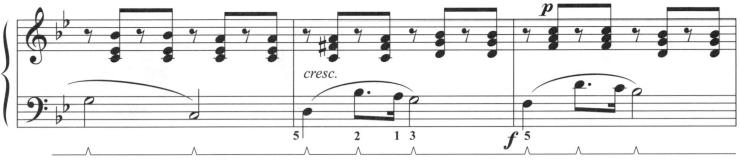

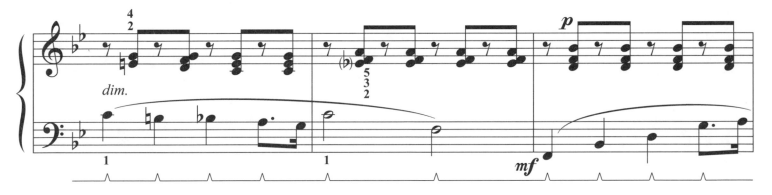

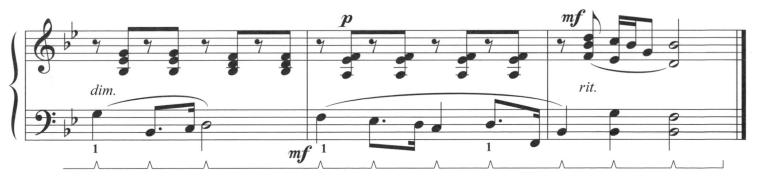

* Jessie L. Gaynor – American woman composer and educator (1865-1921).

Jolly Coppersmith

Carl Peter, Op. 70

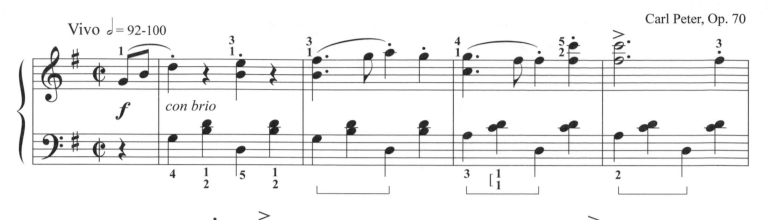

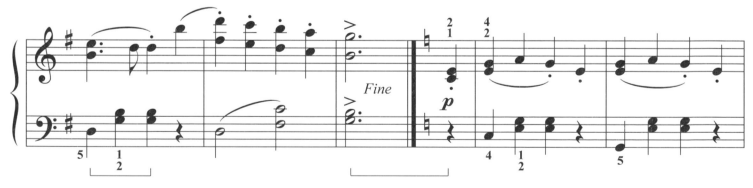

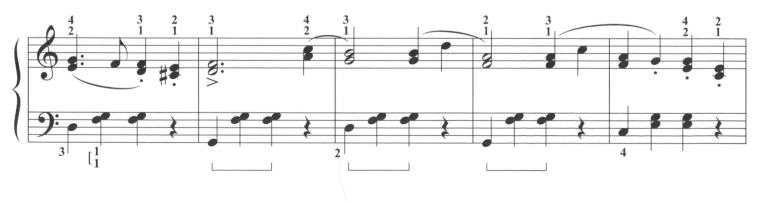

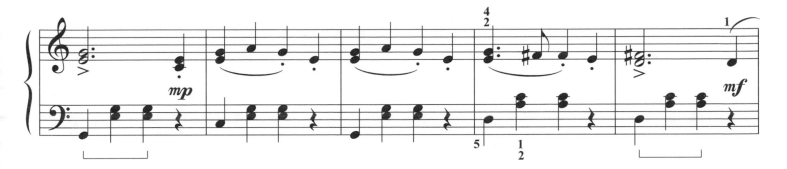

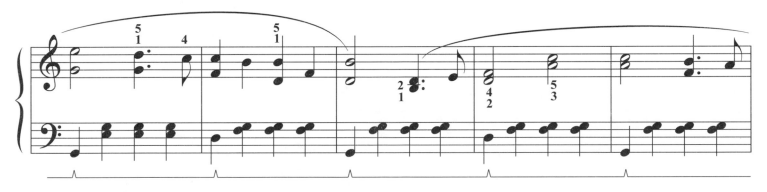

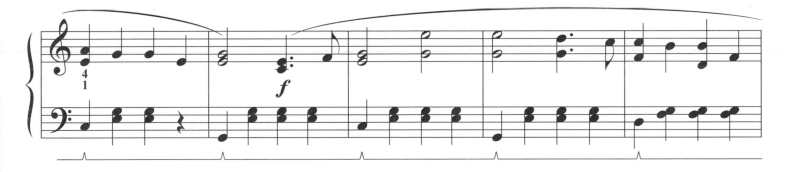

D.C. al Fine

Color It Blue

Blue is a favorite color of many composers. The waltzes in this medley represent two shades of blue.
Blue also describes a sad, wistful mood reflected in *blues style* music incorporating jazz rhythms.

ten. is the abbreviation of **tenuto**, meaning sustained. Notes with this indication should be held to full value.

Valse Bleue (Alfred Margis*)

* Alfred Margis (MAHR-gis) French composer of the late 19th century.

Fingering Note: In the 5th measure of the 3rd line, middle C has the fingering **2-1**. This means you should *change fingering* while holding this note for 3 counts. At first, play middle C with the 2nd finger of R.H., then change to the thumb *while keeping the key down*.

Valse Bluette (R. Drigo*)

Allegro ♩= 138-152

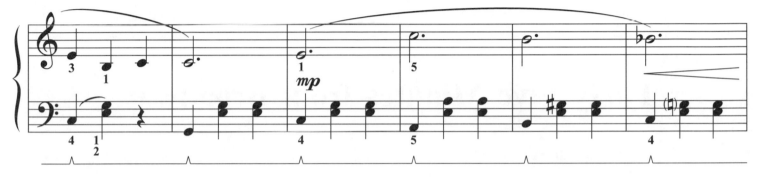

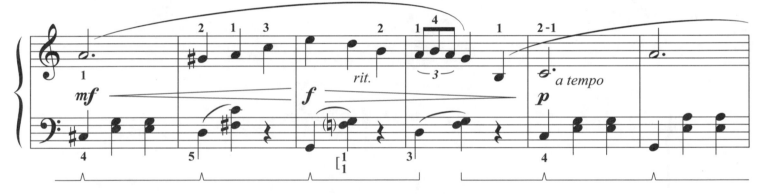

* Riccardo Drigo (DREE-go) Italian piano teacher, composer and conductor of the Russian Imperial Ballet orchestra (1846-1930).

George Michael Cohan was born on the Fourth of July, 1878, in Providence, Rhode Island. His family performed as a musical team in countless vaudeville shows. *Vaudeville* was a live variety show performed on a theater stage. The performance could include magicians, acrobats, standup comedians, skits and various musical groups, including a small orchestra.

Cohan became one of the most popular composers of his time, writing over 500 songs and 150 musical comedy shows. "Yankee Doodle Dandy" and "You're a Grand Old Flag" are among his best known songs.

"Forty-Five Minutes From Broadway" was introduced in a musical comedy of the same name in 1905. Broadway is a famous street in New York City.

Playing Vocal Music – The music on pages 18 and 19 is printed as a vocal solo with piano accompaniment. The *upper* staff of each line is the *voice part*. The pianist plays only the *bottom two staffs*.

The **brace**, which joins the bottom two staffs, will help you to more easily find the piano accompaniment part.

Forty-Five Minutes from Broadway

Tempo di Valse ♩ = 138-152

George M. Cohan (1878-1942)

Only for-ty-five min-utes from Broad - way,

Think of the chang-es it brings. For the short time it

Whole Tone Scale – The whole tone scale is built *entirely of whole steps*. It has a unique exotic sound. There are only two such scales. Although other whole tones scales may use different accidentals or start on a different note, they all sound the same as scale No. 1 or scale No. 2, shown in the Finger Workout below.

Whole tone scale No. 1 is used in "Mexican Clap Hands Dance" and "Yankee Doodle."
Scale No. 2 is used in "Frere Jacques." The last measure of each piece uses notes that are *not* part of the whole tone scale. This is done to make the endings sound more conclusive.

FINGER WORKOUT (Technic Preparatory) – Repeat several times daily.

Whole Tone Scale No. 1   Whole Tone Scale No. 2

Whole Tone Parody

Medley of three familiar tunes using whole tone scales.

Mexican Clap-Hands Dance

Giocoso ♪= 168-184   Wesley Schaum

Frere Jacques

Andante ♩ = 63-72

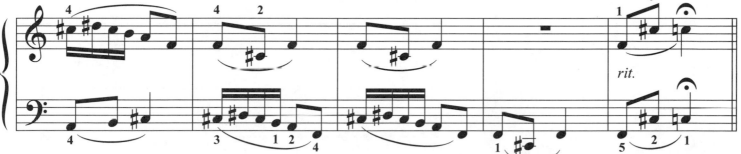

Yankee Doodle

Moderato ♩ = 92-100

basso marcato

U Turn
Permitted Here

A **turn** is a musical ornament which revolves (turns) around a printed note, called the *principal note*. Notice that the turn *begins* on the *note above* the principal note and *ends* on the principal note.

As written: As played:

   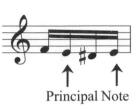

Principal Note   Principal Note

An accidental sign (♯ ♭ or ♮) *below* the turn affects the *lower* note.

In the music below, red arrows connect the turn symbol and the notes which it represents.

Con brio ♩ = 100-112

John W. Schaum

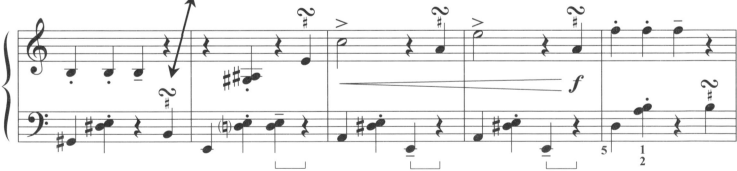

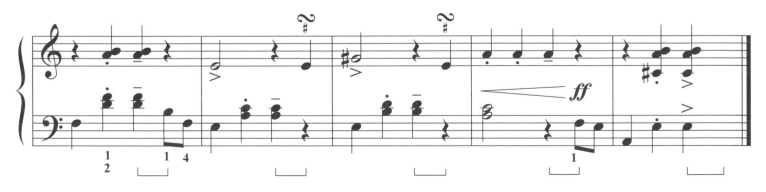

Lake Lucerne

*Jacques-Dalcroze, Op. 5, No. 1

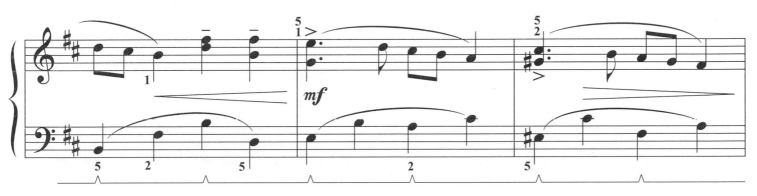

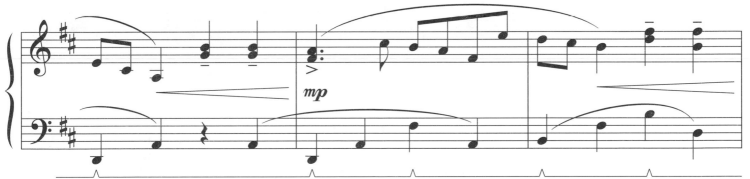

* Emile Jacques-Dalcroze (ay-MEEL zhock-DAHL-crows) was a Swiss composer (1865-1950). He established a famous school and system combining music and rhythmic body movements called "Eurhythmics." This was the forerunner of modern aerobic dancing.

Legend of the Plains

Tremolo is a rapid alternation of the notes of an interval or chord. The tremolo adds excitement and a rumbling effect to music. In this piece, the tremolo is indicated by two half notes connected with a 16th note beam. It means that notes should be alternated at the rate of 16th notes for the duration of the half note. On page 25, in measures 33 through 36, the tremolo notes are written as 16th notes. In measures 41 through 44, the tremolo abbreviation is used.

*Charles Wakefield Cadman, Op. 21

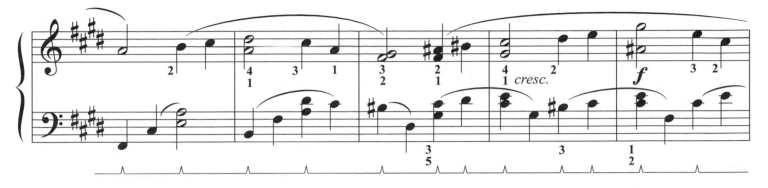

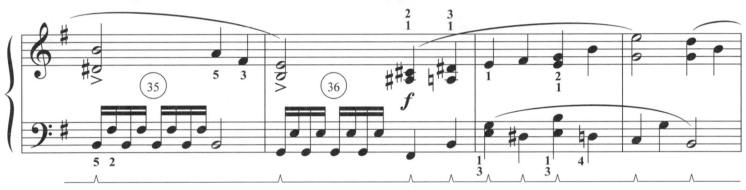
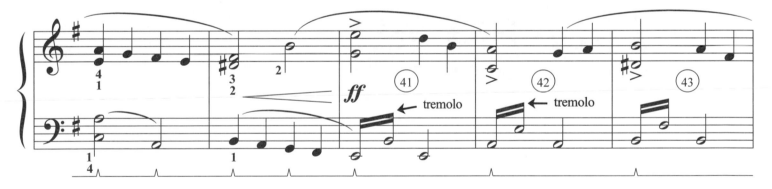
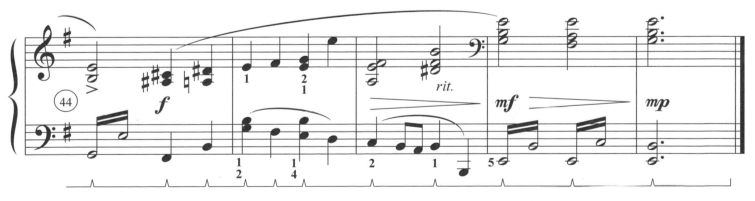

* Charles Wakefield Cadman (1881-1946), American composer, pianist and teacher, born in Johnstown, Pennsylvania. His interest in Native Americans prompted him to record and publish various tribal songs and give a series of lecture-concerts of Native American music. This piece, "Legend of the Plains," is based on Native American music and lore.

La Traviata

An **opera** is a *secular* story set to music with emphasis on singing of vocal solos, ensembles and choruses with orchestral accompaniment. Dancing and ballet sequences are often included. It is staged with a full array of costumes, props, scenery, lighting and special effects.

This piece uses themes from the first act of "La Traviata" by the Italian opera composer, Giuseppi Verdi.

Allegro ♩ = 168-184

Verdi (1813-1901)

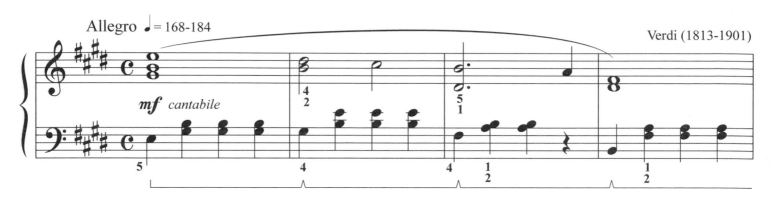

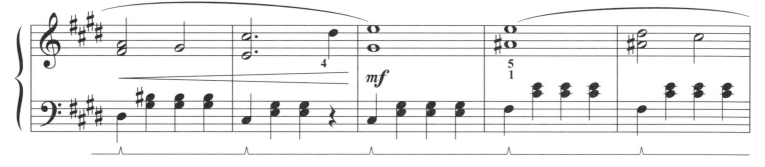

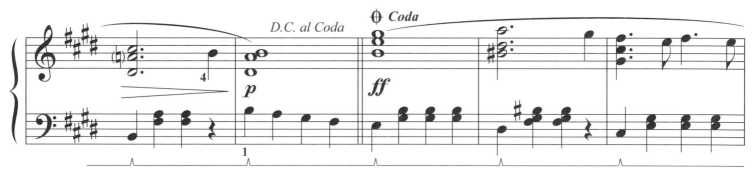

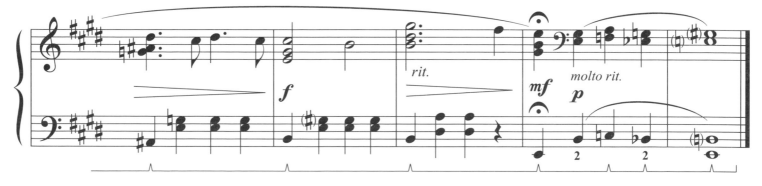

Creation

Hymn and choir music uses music notation with *different note stems* to show the four different voice parts.
Soprano and *alto* parts are in the *treble* staff. Soprano notes have stems UP – alto notes have stems DOWN.
Tenor and *bass* parts are in the *bass* staff. Tenor notes have stems UP – bass notes have stems DOWN.
For preparatory practice, play each voice part separately, starting with soprano and moving downward.

The "Creation" is an **oratorio** – a *religious* story set to music. Like an opera (see page 26), it has vocal solos, ensembles and choruses with orchestral accompaniment. However, an oratorio is performed in a *concert hall*, not a theater. It has no scenery, costumes or props. This piece is a transcription from the original choral-orchestral version. The complete score of Haydn's "Creation" takes over two hours to perform!

* Franz Joseph Haydn (HIGH-den) Great Austrian composer (1732-1809).

Shadow Waltz

32nd Notes are indicated by a *triple beam*. Four 32nd notes fit into the same time space as one 8th note. See the bottom line of pages 28 and 29. In 3/8 time, 32nd notes are counted like this:

Allegretto grazioso ♪ = 104-112

*Meyerbeer

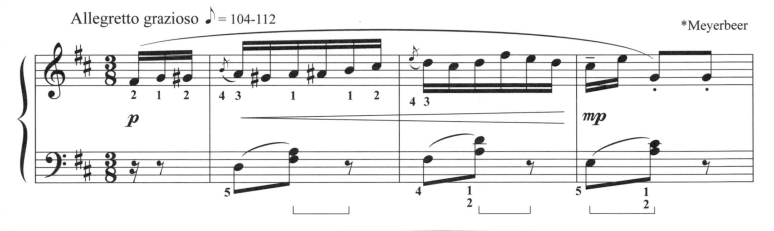

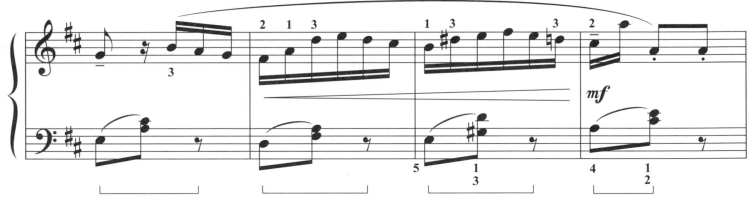

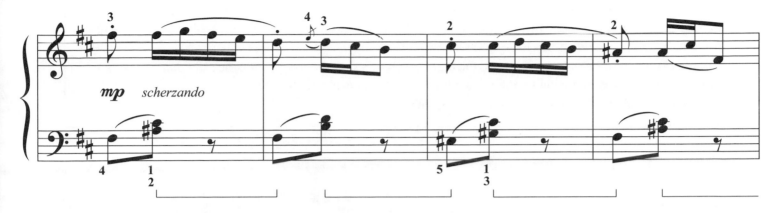

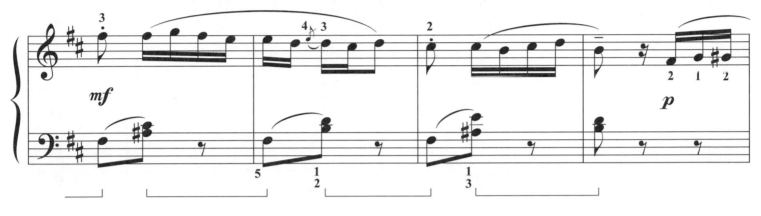

* **Giacomo** (jah-COE-moh) **Meyerbeer** (1791-1864) was a German opera composer. His name was originally Jacob Meyer Beer, but he changed it to improve his image as a composer. The "Shadow Waltz" is a theme from his opera, "Dinorah." This opera is all but forgotten, except for this waltz, which remains a concert favorite and is in the recital repertoire of many coloratura soprano singers.

Suggested supplementary solo books: **Best of Chopin** (catalog #07-13) and **Handel's Messiah** (catalog # 09-25)

Jasmine

Melody and accompaniment in the same hand – The right hand plays *both* melody and accompaniment. In the treble staff, *melody* notes have stems DOWN; *accompaniment* notes have stems UP.

While playing, *tilt* the right hand toward the thumb. This will shift the weight onto the right thumb, making it easier to emphasize the melody notes while playing the accompaniment notes softly.

Be sure to hold the dotted half notes to their full length.

Tempo di valse ♩ = 120-132

Kussner

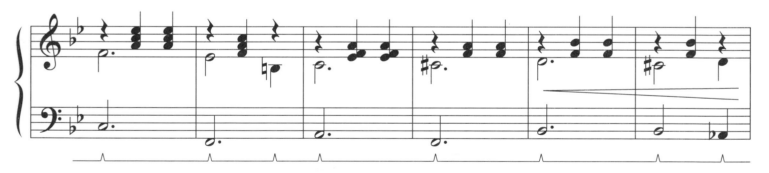

Two Swans

Allegro moderato ♩ = 116-132

*Leschetizky, Op. 2, No. 1

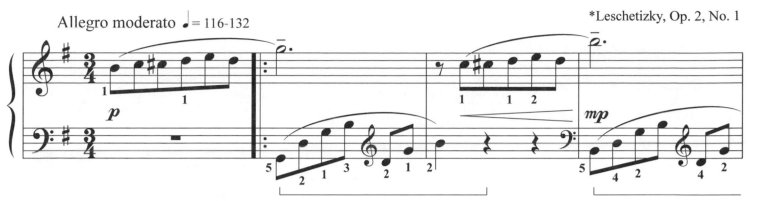

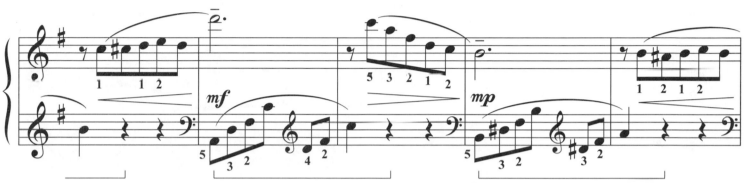

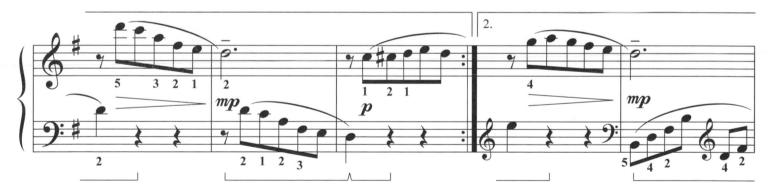

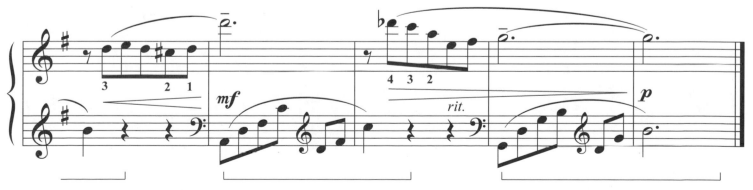

* Theodor Leschetizky (lesh-ih-TISS-key) Famous concert pianist, teacher and composer born in Poland (1830-1915).

Carefree

Allegro con grazia ♩= 160-176

*Dennee, Op. 15 No. 5

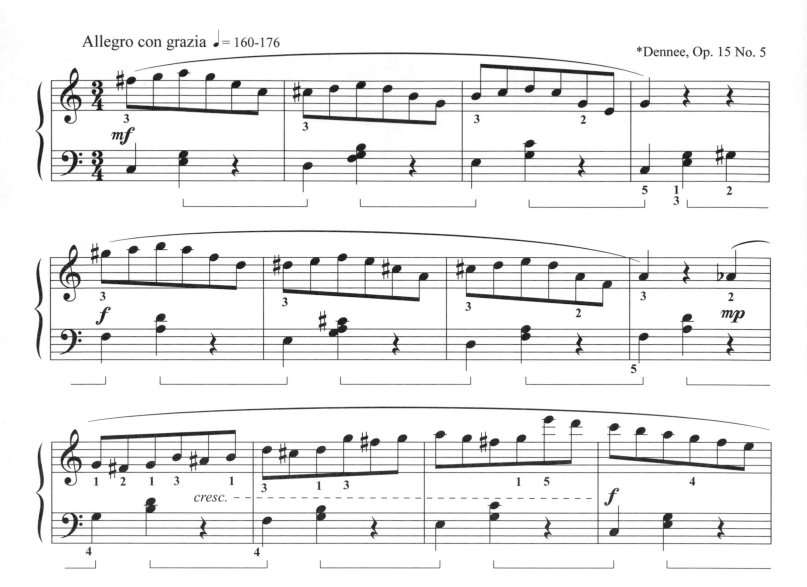

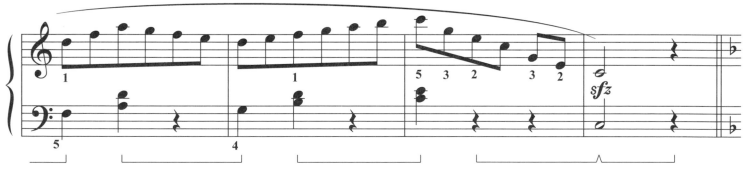

* Charles Dennee (den-NAY) American pianist and composer who taught at the New England Conservatory, played nearly 1100 recitals and wrote children's music and operettas (1863-1946).

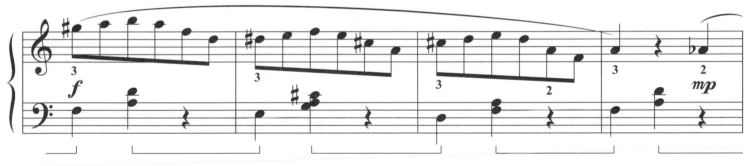

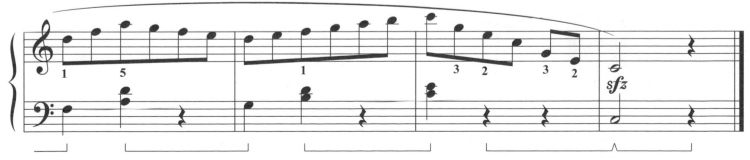

Procession of the Nobles

Maestoso ♩ = 88-96

*Rimsky-Korsakov

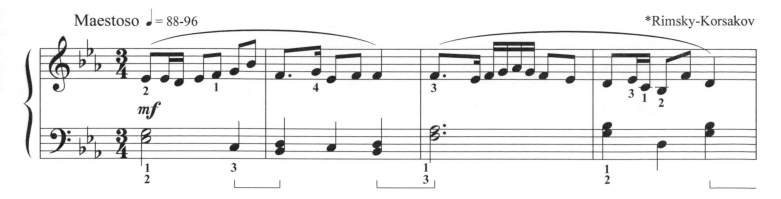

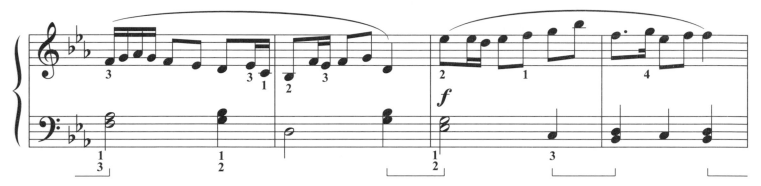

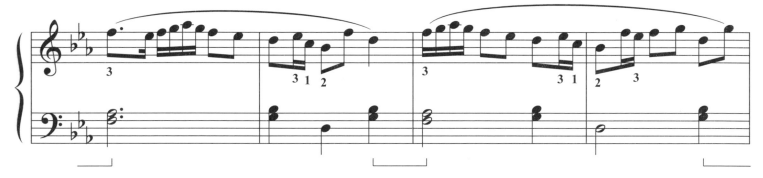

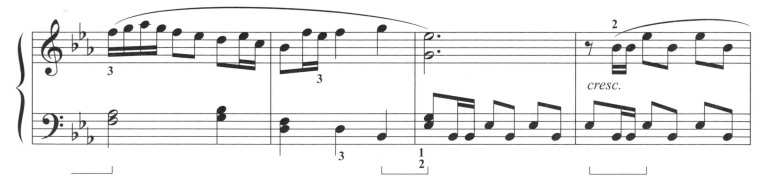

* Nicholas Rimsky-Korsakov (RIM-skee KORE-sah-kov) A prolific Russian composer (1844-1908). He wrote 17 operas and many pieces of orchestral, choral, piano and chamber music. "Procession of the Nobles" is from his opera-ballet, *Mlada*.

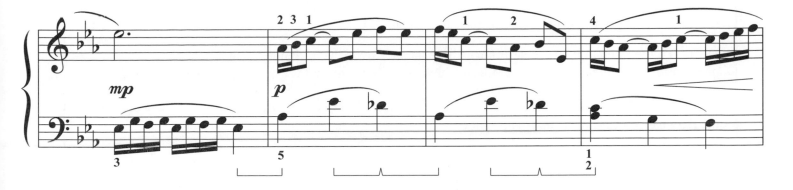

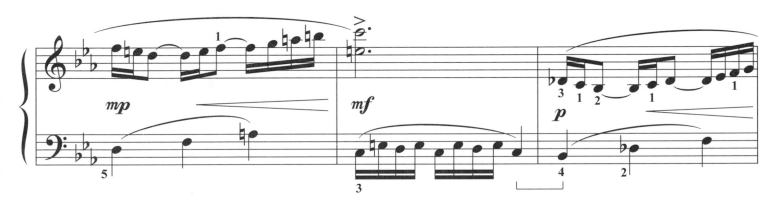

Riderless Horse

The riderless horse walks in a national funeral parade as the symbol of a lost leader. This is done as a memorial tribute to presidents, heads of state and military heros.

DIRECTIONS: The *first two lines* of music have the melody in the TOP notes of the right hand. When playing, *tilt* the right hand toward the 4th and 5th fingers. This will shift the weight of the hand, making it easier to emphasize the upper note melody.

The *last two lines* of music have the melody in the LOWER notes of the right hand. When playing, *tilt* the right hand toward the thumb. This will make it easier to emphasize the lower note melody.

Larghetto

Emphasize TOP notes of right hand. *(Lower notes in treble staff are played with right hand thumb.)*

Crawford

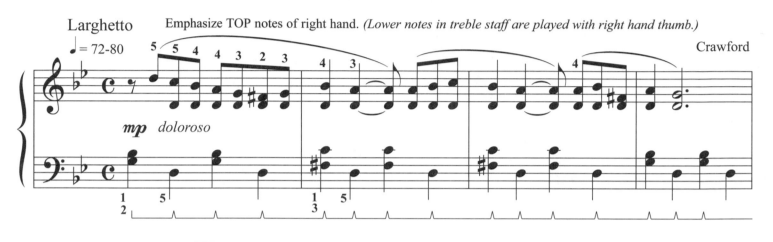

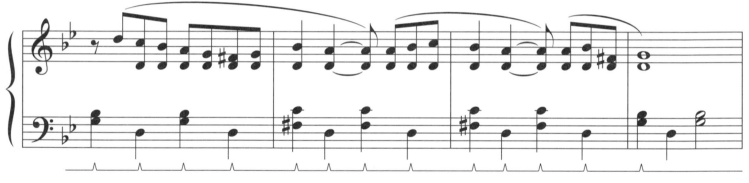

Emphasize LOWER notes of right hand. *(Upper notes in treble staff are played with right hand 5th finger.)*

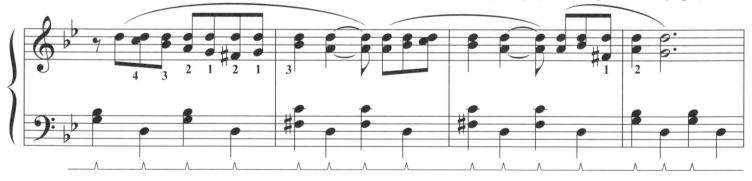

Intermezzo

In this piece, the right hand melody is sometimes the *upper note* and sometimes the *lower note*. This is indicated with red. When playing, *tilt* the hand toward the upper or lower notes, as needed.

* Johannes Brahms (brAHMz) Outstanding German composer (1833-1897).

Green Hills

> **Impressionism** was a style of music and art popular during the late 1800's and early 1900's, especially in France. Its purpose was to convey a mood, somewhat diffused vision or general impression rather than specific descriptive details. It uses free-moving, colorful harmonies and tonalities, often producing a dreamlike atmosphere. It is very different from the formal style of composers such as Bach and Beethoven.

Poco scherzando ♩ = 120–132

*Cyril Scott

39

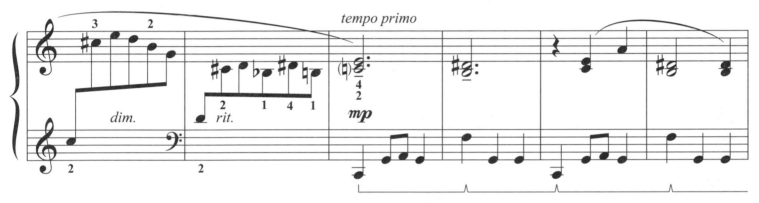

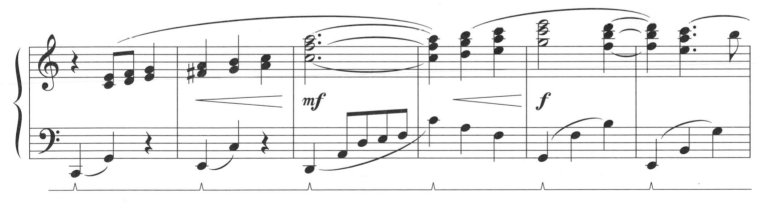

* Cyril Scott was a British impressionistic composer (1879-1970).

Night and Day

A **Two-part Invention** is a type of polyphonic music made famous by Bach. This piece has a short two-measure melody which is repeated many times, both in the right hand and left hand. The melody is sometimes transposed, starting on a different note. In some of the repetitions, the melody notes have been changed slightly.

The melody is indicated by a slur. The first two notes of the melody have accent marks.

For extra ensemble experience, make this piece into a DUET by having the **first person** play the *upper staff* notes in octaves. The left hand plays the upper staff notes as written, the right hand plays the same notes *one octave higher*.

The **second person** plays the *lower staff* notes in octaves. The right hand plays the lower staff notes as written, the left hand plays the same notes *one octave lower*.

Harpsichord Dance Tune

A **mordent** (꙳) is a musical ornament. Its symbol is a short zig-zag *with an added vertical line*. It is played by quickly alternating the principal note with the note one scale degree LOWER.

The symbol for an **inverted mordent** (꙳) is a zig-zag *without* a vertical line. It alternates the principal note with the note one scale degree HIGHER.

Mordent played in measure 19:   **Inverted Mordent** played in measure 4:

Allegretto ♩ = 126-138

Inverted Mordent

*Scarlatti

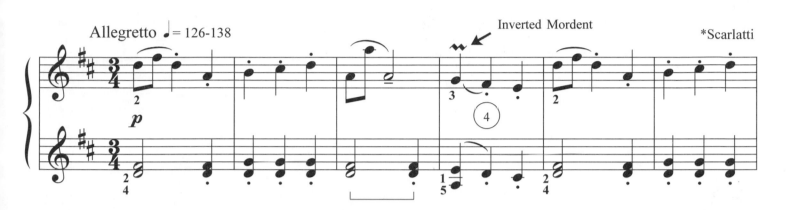

Mordent

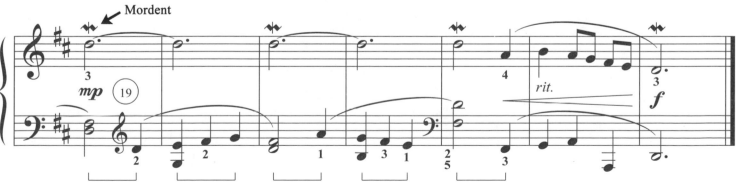

* Domenico Scarlatti (doh-MEN-ee-koh skar-LAH-tee) Celebrated Italian composer (1685-1757). This piece was written for the **harpsichord**, an early keyboard instrument which was the forerunner of the piano.

Note: The interpretation of the mordent and inverted mordent shown here concurs with articles in the "Harvard Dictionary of Music" and in "Grove's Dictionary of Music."

Pursuit

DIRECTIONS: The right hand plays *both melody and accompaniment*. In this piece, melody notes have *double stems* (up and down). As explained on page 36, *tilt* the right hand toward the 4th and 5th fingers to help emphasize the melody notes.

*Per Lasson

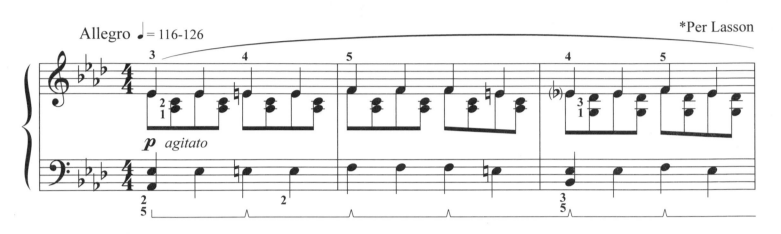

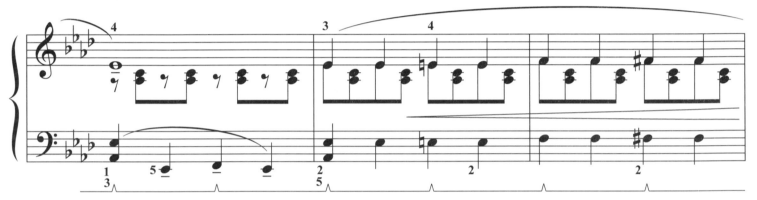

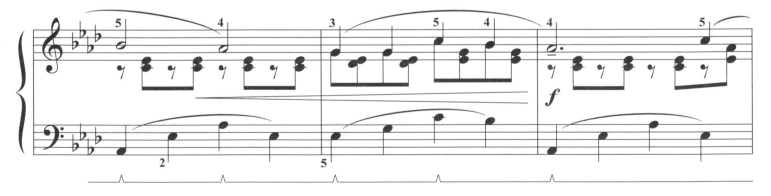

* Per Lasson (LAH-sun) Norwegian composer of vocal and piano works (1859-1883). His father and brother were also composers.

Teacher's Note: It is interesting to compare this piece with "Jasmine" on page 30. There, the melody has the notes with *stems down* and the accompaniment has the notes with *stems up*.

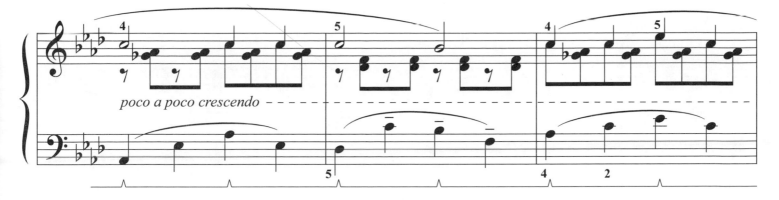

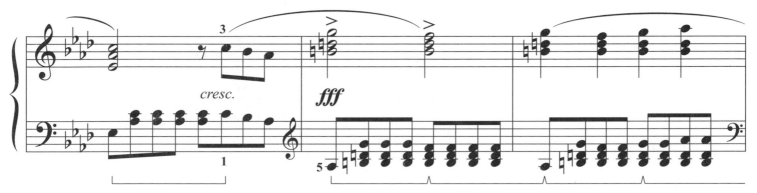

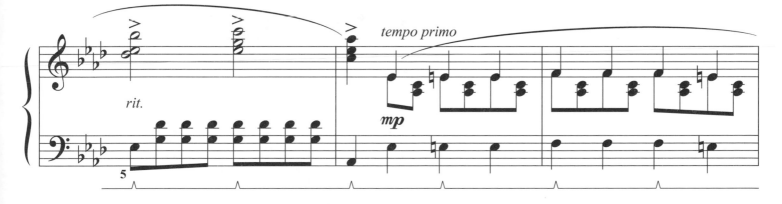

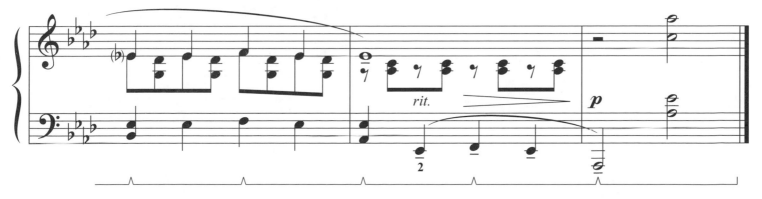

Control Tower

*Wilm, Op. 12 No. 5

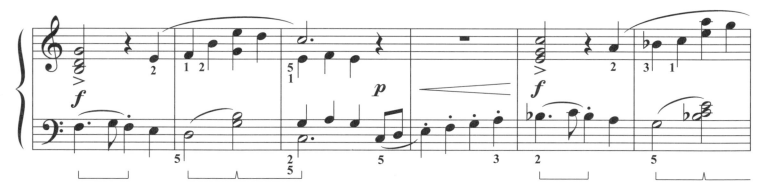

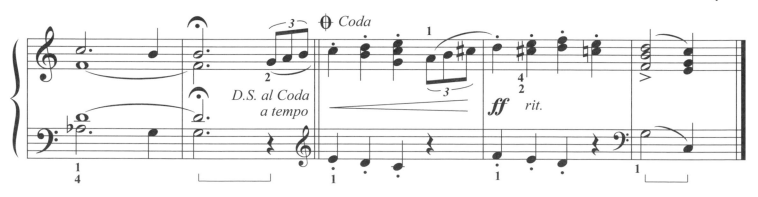

* Nicolai von Wilm, Russian-born composer, pianist and poet (1834-1911). He was educated in Germany where he spent most of his life. He is best known for his chamber music, but he also composed piano music and vocal music.

Making Music Quiz

DIRECTIONS: Match each musical term in the left column with the correct definition in the right column. Write the alphabetical letter of the definition on the proper line next to each number. The first answer is a sample. If necessary, refer to the Reference Page (front inside cover) or the Music Dictionary (page 46).

Date _____   Grade or Score _____

K 1. una corda

A. inverted mordent

____ 2. ∾

B. American woman composer

____ 3. sostenuto

C. staccato accent (martellato)

____ 4. Jacques-Dalcroze

D. hurrying the tempo

____ 5. ⤳

E. tremolo

____ 6. soprano

F. Swiss composer who combined music with rhythmic body movements

____ 7. opera

G. religious story set to music

____ 8. tarantella

H. British impressionistic composer

____ 9. ♪

I. sustaining notes to their full duration

____ 10. Jessie L. Gaynor

J. treble notes with stems up in 4-part choral music

____ 11. ⤳

K. soft pedal

____ 12. ♪

L. Italian opera composer

____ 13. tenor

M. Italian folk dance in 6/8 time

____ 14. stringendo

N. whole tone scale

____ 15. George M. Cohan

O. secular story set to music

____ 16. presto

P. American composer

____ 17. Verdi

Q. mordent

____ 18. oratorio

R. turn

____ 19. Cyril Scott

S. very fast

____ 20. ♪

T. bass notes with stems up in 4-part choral music

Music Dictionary

Terms listed here are limited to those commonly found in Level 5 methods and supplements. Many elementary terms such as *forte* and *piano* are not included because of limited space. Pronunciations have accented syllables shown in capital letters.

For a more complete listing, the *Schaum Dictionary of Musical Terms* is a separate 1500-word compilation especially for keyboard students.

accel. = accelerando (ahk-sell-er-ON-doh) Becoming gradually faster in tempo.

adagio (ah-DAH-jee-oh) Slow, slowly.

affettuoso (ah-fet-too-OH-soh) Affectionately.

agitato (ahd-jih-TAH-toh) Agitated, restless.

allegretto (ah-leh-GRET-toh) A little slower than *allegro*.

alto (AL-toh) Low female voice. See page 27.

andante (ahn-DAHN-tay) Moderately slow.

andantino (ahn-dahn-TEE-noh) A little faster than *andante*.

animato (ah-nee-MAH-toh) Lively, spirited.

a tempo (ah TEHM-poh) Return to the previous tempo.

bass 1) Low male voice. 2) Lowest sounding pitch. See pg. 27.

basso marcato (BAH-so mahr-CAH-toh) Emphasize notes in the bass staff.

cantabile (cahn-TAH-bil-lay) Singing style.

cantando (cahn-TAHN-doh) Singing style.

chromatic (kro-MAH-tik) Series of notes proceeding by half steps.

coda (KOH-dah) Extra musical section at the end of a piece. Often indicated by the symbol: ⊕

con brio (kone BREE-oh) With vigor, spirit, gusto.

con moto (kone MOH-toh) With motion, movement.

D.C. = da capo (dah KAH-poh) Return to the beginning and repeat.

D.C. al coda Return to the beginning and repeat until *To Coda*. Then skip to ⊕ *Coda* and play to the end of piece.

D.C. al fine (ahl FEE-nay) Return to the beginning and repeat, ending at the word *Fine*.

dolce (DOL-chay) Sweetly, softly.

doloroso (doh-loh-ROH-soh) Sadly, sorrowfully.

drammatico (dreh-MAH-tee-koh) Dramatic.

D.S. = dal segno (dahl SEN-yo) Return to the sign 𝄋 and repeat.

D.S. al coda Return to the sign 𝄋 and repeat until *To Coda*. Then skip to ⊕ *Coda* and play to the end of the piece.

D.S. al fine Return to the sign 𝄋 and repeat, ending at the word *Fine*.

espressivo (ehs-pres-SEE-voh) With expression and emotion.

𝆑𝆑𝆑 = fortississimo (fohr-tih-SISS-ee-moh) Extremely loud.

15ᵐᵃ = Play the notes two octaves *higher* than written.

fine (FEE-nay) End. (see *D.C. al fine* and *D.S. al fine*)

giocoso (jee-oh-KOH-soh) Humorously, playfully.

grazia (GRAHT-zee-ah) Grace, elegance.

grazioso (graht-zee-OH-soh) Gracefully.

impressionism Style of music. See page 38.

intermezzo (inn-ter-MET-zoh) Musical interlude. See page 37.

inverted mordent (MOR-dent) Musical ornament indicated by the sign: ↝ See page 41.

larghetto (lahr-GET-oh) Tempo a little faster than *largo*.

largo (LAHR-goh) Very slow, solemn.

leggiero (led-jee-AIR-oh) Light, delicate. Abbreviation: *legg.*

lento (LEN-toh) Slow, but not as slow as *largo*.

maestoso (my-ess-TOH-soh) Majestic, dignified, proudly.

martellato (mahr-tel-LAH-toh) Heavy staccato accent indicated by the sign: ▼ See page 9.

meno mosso (MAY-noh MOHS-soh) Less motion, less quickly.

𝆐𝆑 = mezzo forte (MET-zoh FOHR-tay) Medium loud. Softer than *forte*.

molto (MOHL-toh) Very, much.

mordent (MOR-dent) Musical ornament indicated by the sign: ↝ See page 41.

𝆐𝆏 = mezzo piano (MET-zoh pee-YAH-noh) Medium soft. Louder than *piano*.

non troppo (nohn TROHP-poh) Not too much.

op. = opus (OH-puss) Unit of musical work usually numbered in chronological order. May be a composition of any length, from a short single piece to a full symphony.

opera (AH-per-ah) Secular musical drama. See page 26.

oratorio (or-ah-TOH-ree-oh) Musical drama based on a *religious* story or text. See page 27.

passione (pah-see-OH-neh) Passion, emotion.

pesante (peh-SAHN-teh) Heavy, weighty.

piu mosso (PEE-oo MOHS-soh) More motion, faster.

poco (POH-koh) Little.

poco a poco (POH-koh ah POH-koh) Little by little, gradually.

𝆏𝆏𝆏 = pianississimo (pee-ah-nih-SISS-ee-moh) Extremely soft.

presto (PRESS-toh) Very fast. Faster than *allegro*.

program music Descriptive music. See page 4.

scherzando (skare-TSAHN-doh) Playfully, jokingly.

semplice (SEMM-plee-chay) Simple, plain.

𝆑𝆎 = sforzando (sfor-TSAHN-doh) Sudden emphasis or accent on a note or chord.

soprano (soh-PRAH-noh) High female voice. See page 27.

sostenuto (soss-teh-NOO-toh) Sustained, holding notes to full value.

stringendo (strin-JEN-doh) Accelerating.

tarantella (tair-an-TELL-ah) Italian folk dance. See page 6.

tempo di valse (TEHM-poh dih VALSZ) Waltz time.

tempo primo (TEHM-poh PREE-moh) Return to the original tempo.

ten. = tenuto (teh-NOO-toh) Sustained, held to full value.

tenor High male voice. See page 27.

tranquillo (trahn-KWILL-oh) Tranquil, quiet.

tremolo (TREHM-uh-loh) Trembling effect produced by rapidly alternating notes or chord tones. See page 24.

turn Musical ornament, symbol: ∾ See page 22.

una corda (OO-nah KOHR-dah) Use the soft pedal on a piano. Literally: *one string*.

vivace (vee-VAH-chay) Lively, quick.

vivo (VEE-voh) Lively, animated.

Certificate of Progress

This certifies that

_____

has successfully completed

LEVEL FIVE

of the Schaum
Making Music Method

and is eligible for advancement to
LEVEL SIX

Schaum

_____
Teacher

_____
Date

Successful Schaum Sheet Music

This is a Partial List — Showing Level 5 through Level 7

• = Original Form   ✓ = Chord Symbols

ANIMALS
67-23 • OF A TAILOR AND A BEAR .... MacDowell 6

BOOGIE
64-06   COTTON PICKIN' BOOGIE .... Myddleton 5
67-21 • DEEP RHYTHM (Boogie Style) .... Reisfeld 6
64-29   IN THE HALL of the BOOGIE KING ..... Grieg/Schaum 5

CHRISTMAS
70-11   CAROL of the BELLS .... Ukranian Bell Carol 6
70-03   CHRISTMAS FANTASY .... Medley 6
67-02   GREENSLEEVES (6/8 Time) .... Cameo Transcription 6
67-15   I WONDER AS I WANDER .... Appalachian Carol 6
70-13   JAZZY OLD ST. NICHOLAS .... Arr. W. Schaum 5
70-04   JINGLE BELLS JUBILEE .... Theme & Variations 6
67-18   RISE UP SHEPHERDS, AND FOLLOW .... Spiritual 6
67-06   TOYLAND .... Herbert 6

CIRCUS
64-36   CIRCUS GRAND MARCH ("Entry of the Gladiators") .... Fucik 5

CLASSICS
67-16 • Bach .... COMPUTER INVENTION (2-Part, No. 13) 6
64-05   Chopin ....ETUDE IN E MAJOR 5
67-20   Clementi .... CONVERSATION WALTZ 6
69-02   Dvorak ...... HUMORESQUE (Concert Transcription) 7
64-04   Handel ....HALLELUJAH CHORUS 5
64-16 • Heller .... CURIOUS STORY 5
67-17   Pachelbel .... CANON 6
67-01   Rossini .... LA DANZA (6/8 Time) 6
64-02   Saint-Saens .... DANSE MACABRE 5
67-07   Schubert .... AVE MARIA (Cameo Transcription) 6
64-09 ✓ Strauss .... BLUE DANUBE 5
64-35   Tchaikowsky . MARCH from 6th SYMPHONY (3rd Mvt) 5

COUNTRY/WESTERN
64-41 • RAWHIDE .... Cahn 5

DESCRIPTIVE MUSIC
64-44 • NORDIC SPRING .... Cahn 5
64-22 • REFLECTIONS .... Cahn 5
64-23   STORM, The (Minor Key) .... Pitcher 5
64-31 • SUMMER NOCTURNE .... Levin 5
64-24 • TWO MOODS (Major - Minor) .... Cahn 5
64-30 • VIENNA REMEMBERED .... Cahn 5

DISSONANCE
67-14 • SOUVENIR (Quartal-Quintal Harmony) .... Croom 6
64-20 • TOKEN (Quartal-Quintal Harmony) .... Croom 5

DUETS (1 Piano, 4 Hands)
71-06   BEETHOVEN'S 6th SYMPHONY ...... (2nd Mvt. Theme) 5
71-04   RONDO IN A MAJOR, Op. 107 .... Schubert 5
71-05   SLAVONIC DANCE in E-Minor, Op. 72 .... Dvorak 6

FLOWERS
64-28 • GENTLE BLOSSOM .... Cahn 5

JAZZ STYLE
67-24   BLUE VELVET .... Hudson 6
64-15 • CLOWNING AROUND .... King 5
64-38 • ROCK RHAPSODY (Syncopated 3/4 Time) .... King 5
64-37 • SNAZZY .... Weston 5

LATIN AMERICAN
67-22 • FIESTA EN ESPANA (Minor Key) .... Cahn 6
69-01   MEXICAN HAT DANCE .... Concert Transcription 7

MARCHES
67-05   MARCH of the TOYS (Grace Notes) .... Herbert 6

MINOR KEY
64-34 • CONTEMPLATION .... Cahn 5

RAGTIME
64-25 ✓ ALEXANDER'S RAGTIME BAND .... Berlin 5

ROMANTIC MOOD
67-08   CLAIR DE LUNE (Key of C Major) .... Debussy 6
64-22 • REFLECTIONS .... Cahn 5
64-32 • ROMANCE .... Levin 5
64-33   SERENADE .... Herbert 5
64-31 • SUMMER NOCTURNE .... Levin 5

SACRED
64-45   AMAZING GRACE .... Arr. Cupp 5
64-40   IT IS WELL WITH MY SOUL .... Bliss / Arr. Cupp 5
64-49   REFLECTIONS of the CROSS (medley) ..... Arr. Cupp 5
64-43   STAND UP, STAND UP FOR JESUS .... Arr. Cupp 5
64-42   SWEET HOUR OF PRAYER .... Bradbury / Arr. Cupp 5

SHOWY DISPLAY SOLOS
64-13 • AVALANCHE .... Heller 5
67-12   FIREWORKS (Grace Notes) .... Ponchielli 6
64-39 • POWERHOUSE .... Schaum 5
67-11 • SOLFEGGIETTO .... C.P.E. Bach 6

SONATINA
64-26 • RUSTIC SONATINA .... Armstrong 5

TV THEME
67-19   TRUMPET FANFARE (used in "Masterpiece Theater") ... 6